Ancient Aliens

By Sean Keyhoe

***

Ancient Aliens

By Sean Keyhoe

Table of Contents

Introduction

The topic of Ancient Aliens has recently exploded in popularity. Due in large part to a number of books and popular television programs on the subject, people are curious as to whether we may have been visited by extra-terrestrials in our distant past.

It seems from today's perspective that recorded history has sprung up quite recently in the time scale of history. It is difficult to find detailed ancient writing that dates beyond 3500 B.C. and it is quite certain that there are virtually no definitive written historical documents in a discernible language that date beyond 5000 B.C.

With such a short period of recorded history, one wonders whether the organized civilization of humanity was helped along somehow by the sudden introduction of technology from extra-terrestrial beings. Such a theory certainly provides a huge area for speculation, wonder and research.

In this book I have attempted to present a wide range of ideas and topics that persistently arise when examining the question of ancient aliens. I hope you find this information to be as thought-provoking, compelling and thoroughly fascinating as I have in my quest for ancient alien discovery.

~ Sean Keyhoe 2014

Chapter 1 - Ancient UFO Sightings

Since the dawn of civilization people have gazed in wonder at the night sky. As humans watched the mesmerizing movements of the stars across the black canopy of space, they discovered that the changing patterns of the stars precisely matched the changing seasons on Earth. This allowed them to create calendars and plan ahead for the cultivation of crops.

But some objects in the sky did not follow a regular path or any orderly pattern. These objects seemed to defy the predictable patterns of the stars. These unidentified flying objects, or UFO's, posed a challenge for human understanding and initiated a challenge that continues to this day.

Despite the current popularity of the theory that UFO's may have been visiting the Earth in the distant past, many people, including most of the scientific community are still overwhelmingly skeptical about the topic. Ancient peoples saw weird things in the sky and they explained them as gods since they felt their lives were controlled by the gods. In most cases it is not difficult to propose more than one explanation. These ancient peoples may not have understood cosmic events like meteors or comets; it could have been any number of things that were unknown by primitive societies but these ancient societies explained them as supernatural events.

Even though a large portion of these ancient recorded events can be explained, there are still many that defy explanation. One of the earliest written records of an encounter with a UFO comes from Ancient Egypt. There is a story about an Egyptian Pharaoh who saw circles of fire in the sky. At first he saw one but then a few days later, there were many in the sky. The Pharaoh was so impressed that he had details of the event recorded on a papyrus. Excerpts of the translation read as follows:

"In the year 22, of the third month of winter, sixth hour of the day [...] among the scribes of the House of Life it was found that a strange Fiery Disk was coming in the sky. ...

After several days had passed, they became more numerous in the sky than ever. They shined in the sky more than the brightness of the sun, and extended to the limits of the four supports of heaven [...] Powerful was the position of the Fiery Disks.

... And it was [ordered] that the event [be recorded for] His Majesty in the Annals of the House of Life [to be remembered] forever."

– The records of Pharaoh Tuthmosis 1480 B.C.[1]

The working hypotheses for historians for hundreds of years has always been that mankind is alone in the universe, that there are no intruders from outer space, that there were no advanced civilizations beyond our own and that our civilization is the most advanced. If you cling to those assumptions, there is

---

[1] R. Cedric Leonard – 'Strange Aircraft Over Egypt'

great difficulty to explain many of these old accounts many of which are truly mystifying.

As we continue through history we find more and more detailed accounts of UFO's up until today. It has reached a point where the tide of opinion has shifted to where most believe there 'must be something' that is behind all these UFO reports; they cannot all be explained away.

Chapter 2 - Origin of Ancient Alien Theory

The hypothesis about Earth being visited by ancient aliens is becoming more and more popular due to the many television programs and books that explore this idea. This hypothesis about our distant past would begin with an alien spacecraft approaching Earth and finding homo-sapiens in a state of primitive and uncivilized existence. In terror and wonder, these primitive peoples would watch the descent of these fiery 'gods' from heaven. The spacecraft would have landed, explored Earth, performed strange deeds and then left. To this day, the tales of their visits are related by various cultures in their own unique stories and legends.

This theory really exploded in popularity when the book 'Chariots of the Gods' was written by the Swiss author Erich Von Daniken.

"I tried to prove that this planet was visited by beings from outer space several times in antiquity. Second, I say that one these first visits was the reason why homo-sapiens have become intelligent; so they mated with our fore-fathers and caused a kind of artificial mutation. And finally these visits from outer space have gone into all religions, into mythology and even in some cases into archaeological artifacts." – Erich Von Daniken

It is known that Daniken has sold millions of books all over the world and he continues to be extremely popular even though many of his theories have been countered with contrary opinion and research.

His appeal may be in part because of his continual challenging of generally accepted history. Although his theories may be scorned by traditional scientists, they have certainly found an audience with the general public.

Daniken has spent a lot of time travelling the world looking for evidence to support his theories. People are intrigued by his findings and many suspect that the traditional view of world history may have many errors.

What makes Daniken's views so popular? One person who studied his popularity and was himself an expert on the topic of extra-terrestrial intelligence was the late Carl Sagan.

"We are thinking beings, we are interested and excited in understanding how the world is put together. We seek out the extra-ordinary and if you think of these claims, if only they were true, they would be amazingly interesting; that we have been visited by beings from elsewhere who not only have created our civilization for us but mated with human beings...in my view much more likely to have mated with a Petunia than an extra-terrestrial...but certainly there is a degree of fascination if such accounts were true." – Carl Sagan

Von Daniken has had a thick skin towards such wry skepticism.

"I accept and admit that this theory will not convince conservative scientists but this has always been like this; there is not one simple theory which today is true which has convinced in those days the scientists. Take for example when the first cave paintings were discovered in Spain in the caves and other places; the whole archaeological world were against it; they all said, 'it must be a fake, it's wrong'. Well it's not. It takes usually a generation or ten or twenty years until a new theory will be accepted." – Erich Von Daniken

Time seems to have strangely vindicated Daniken to some extent as the core of his theories are as popular today as they ever have been.

Not all of Daniken's theories have survived scrutiny of course. The pyramids for example - Daniken claimed they could not have been constructed without the help of extra-terrestrial intelligence.

The constructions of the pyramids we now know are generally accepted to be a culmination of a long process of trial and error. Two hundred years before construction began at Giza the Egyptians built structures on the edge of the Nile to be used as tombs. They were underground chambers called Mastabas built of sun-dried mud bricks. From these simple tombs developed the true pyramids but the first were at Saqqara and were stepped pyramids such as the pyramid of King Joseph.

The pyramid of King Joseph was an early pyramid design with tombs and passages underneath. A small stepped pyramid was built on top and then a second larger pyramid was added leaving the structure that exists to this day. This was to become the model for all future pyramids.

The design of Joseph's pyramid owes its strength to the design of the buttressed walls that lean inwards to the center, but the next pyramid built was not as successful. The Egyptians tried to build a pyramid with a much steeper design but the exterior collapsed into a heap of rubble. Through trial and error, they came up with the optimal angle that is found on the great pyramid at Giza with which we are most familiar. Some will still argue that they could not have succeeded without help from extra-terrestrial intelligence but the theory is difficult to support.

So even though some of Daniken's theories have been disputed, no one can deny that he has been instrumental in popularizing the theory of ancient alien contact. Through his determined and consistent promotion, he has probably done more to bring ancient alien theory to a mass audience than any other individual in history.

To get a solid background on opposing theories, the reader is recommended to view the excellent documentary produced by Chris White[2] that refutes

---

[2] Ancientaliensdebunked.com – Chris White with commentary

many of the stated claims by some current popular ancient alien theorists.

---

from Dr. Michael Heiser.

Chapter 3 - Ancient Artifacts

Artifacts discovered throughout the world often display a silent testimony about the history of a civilization and how they tried to understand celestial events. For example there is the great ceremonial center known as Tiwanaku in Bolivia. A part of this site is also known as Puma Punku.

Not as old or as imposing as the pyramids of Egypt, what makes this site so unusual is its unique location. Some believe that it also could not have been built without the influence of a superior intelligence.

Similar to the blocks at Giza, there are huge blocks of stone at Tiwanaku weighing over 100 tons that were transported over 10 kilometers from the source quarries. The huge stones were used to create enormous constructions over 12,000 feet above sea level in an area where it's almost not possible to grow any food. The altitude is so high that the crops come out of the ground stunted. The Tiwanaku had knowledge of advanced agricultural methods that allowed them to grow crops in spite of the harsh conditions.

The structure in the image below has a central figure carved on it of Viracocha, an ancient pre-Inca deity that the peoples of Tiwanaku believed came up from the sea.

The Gate of the Sun at Tiwanaku, Bolivia

We are told that this was accomplished by large labor forces pulling on ropes to haul these huge stones over land but one wonders if there were 'Nephilim' or giants that existed at that time who were able to help move these stones from one location to another. The Tiwanaku who thrived from roughly the time of 300 A.D. to 900 A.D. may have been trying to contact extra-terrestrials with their complex creations and amazing structures. They died out around 1000 A.D. from extended drought.

***

Then there are the Nazca lines in Peru. Covering more than 200 square miles, a bewildering pattern of gigantic artwork litters the Nazca plateau. In additional to images of birds, spiders and animals, narrow straight lines stretch out to every point on the compass. Even though it is likely that these lines represent expressions of their culture, it is hard to understand why someone would make a design so large that it can only be appreciated from the sky.

These lines and images are only clearly visible from the air; at ground level you can only see the subtle alignment and removal of stones on the ground.

A Nazca line at ground level

The Nazca lines are estimated to have been made from between 400 A.D. to 650 A.D.

Aerial view of Nazca Lines

These images may have been created with the intent to communicate with extra-terrestrials that were observed in the sky.

These are really quite remarkable surface sculptures that were essentially made by simply moving small rocks and pebbles that has the effect of changing the color tone of the surface of the desert. It appears that most of these line patterns are oriented towards the heavens in some way. The exact purpose as to why these were created is unknown but one can speculate that it relates to their culture and traditions.

Perhaps the Nazcans were projecting these images into the sky and using them for religious and ceremonial purposes. Perhaps they were made by just a handful of ambitious artists from the Nazca society. The Nazca lines really do constitute a mystery since no one really knows for certain what they were for. Like so much of the ancient world, they remain a silent statement of past activity. Time has hidden the secrets of the exact reason of their creation.

There have been many artifacts discovered that appear to be influenced by extra-terrestrials. For example here is a piece of ancient Mayan jewelry that looks like an aircraft of some type.

Or this Mayan artifact that looks like an astronaut:

Mayan Sculpture from Tikal, Guatemala

But some have argued that the airplane is simply a stylized fish, bird or other animal and the astronaut is simply a ceremonial mask of some sort. It is difficult to find definitive proof since ancient cultures produced such a variety of strange objects most of which were simply a reflection of their natural understanding and customs. Some of their creations are quite impressive in size and the skill needed to produce them. For example:

Olmec Culture, Mexico

This massive stone face was discovered in Mexico. Carved from obsidian, these sculptures were created by the Teotihuacan people. They reached a population of over 200,000 in the range of 1000 B.C. and were located 30 miles northeast of Mexico City. They build the

Pyramid of the sun which had a 720 foot base and was 200 feet tall. It was almost as tall as the great pyramid of Giza.

It is difficult to find definitive proof of ancient alien influence from artifacts partly because there are so many fraudulent claims made in this area. Crystal skulls, ancient writings, obscure treasures of all kinds have been faked by nefarious individuals throughout history. Separating fact from fiction takes time and careful in-depth study.

An ancient artifact that caught my eye while researching this book can be found in the Metropolitan Museum of Art in New York City. This ancient drum is from Peru and can be seen in the image below:

2nd-1st century B.C. - Peru[3]

This ancient drum depicts a humanoid figure

with an exaggerated head on the top. Of particular

---

[3] Drum [Peru; Paracas] (1979.206.1097) In *Heilbrunn Timeline of Art History* . New York: The Metropolitan Museum of Art, 2000–. http://www.metmuseum.org/toah/works-of-art/1979.206.1097. (October 2006)

interest is the shape of the head with pointed protrusions for the nose and ears, no neck and a slit for the mouth.

This 'alien' type of figure matches precisely with one of the most compelling cases of alien abduction of modern times - that of the Pascagoula incident.[4] Charlie Hickson gave a description of an alien creature that he encountered in 1973. He is an artist's depiction:

---

[4] UFO Contact at Pascagoula by Charles Hickson and William Mendez 1983 – page 64. See bonus chapter for additional details.

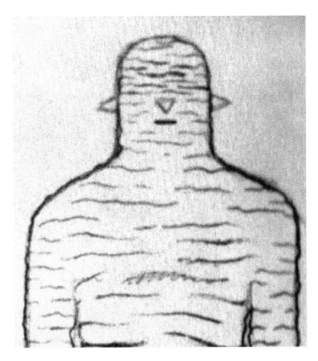

This is the kind of similarity that could confirm evidence of ancient alien contact. A lot of technological capability of ancient societies is difficult to attribute to extra-terrestrial influence but we should expect to see cases of alien representation in their art that parallels what we experience today. Of course some feel that the sudden development of civilized society as a whole could not have occurred without extra-terrestrial intervention.

Regardless of the overall large scale theories, this particular example of the 'no-neck' style of alien creature strikes me as a powerful possibility of the depiction of an alien creature in ancient society.

Chapter 4 - More Historical & Ancient Details

In ancient Egypt, in the city of Abydos in the Temple of Seti I, an inscription was made with objects that look like a submarine, a spacecraft and a helicopter. What these objects are remains a mystery. These hieroglyphs are dated to approximately 1294 B.C. to 1279 B.C.

Hieroglyphs from Ancient Egypt

Close up 1 – Helicopter

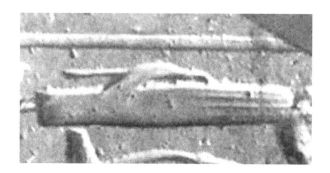

Close up 2 - Submarine

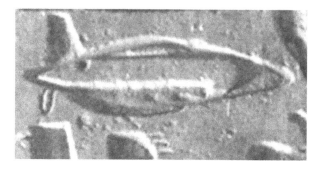

Close up 3 – Spacecraft

Sometimes we have to be careful that we don't trick ourselves into seeing what we want to see. The above images are a good example. Let's look at the helicopter again:

Notice first of all that the 'propeller' touches the tail section; no helicopter is going to get very far if the rotor touches the tail. Secondly, what if we are actually looking at the side view of a tomb? It this next image, an Egyptian coffin image has been superimposed on the original image:

Could it be that the artist who carved the hieroglyphs was simply trying to portray a coffin or a sarcophagus? We could see the second image as a scarab and the third image as a fish but since we are looking for alien images our mind can trick us into seeing what we want to see.

Another example would be the cover of this book. The image from the cover appears to be an ancient Egyptian presenting an offering to an alien being; yet under certain lighting and highlighting, it also appears to simply be a tall vase or receptacle containing plants of some sort:

It is clear that in examining the ancient alien question we need to remain objective and try and avoid seeing what we are want to see or expect to see and instead try to see the truth in a particular situation that may very well be hidden just beneath the surface or beyond our initial impression. It is natural to associate images to those things with which we are familiar in our current culture. It is safe to say that there were probably no helicopters around in the time of ancient Egypt; those masons and craftsmen were most likely making images of things with which they were familiar in their culture at that time in history.

When someone states the 'fact' that there are images of helicopters on ancient Egyptian tombs, it has a tendency to get repeated over and over again; especially in today's 'viral' world. What ends up happening is that you get a case of alternate history or pseudo-history being formed in the mind of the public. That is a polite way to describe a record of history that is simply wrong. The problem is of course that sometimes a version of history comes down to opinion; we can look at the historical facts and come to two totally different conclusions depending on bias, pre-conceived notions and so on and so forth.

Chapter 5 - Space Mysteries and UFO Shapes

In March of 1972 pioneer 10 took off on a journey to the stars, it carried with it a message from the people of Earth. On board is a plaque that tells who we are and where we live, our calling card to the stars. Pioneer has since left our solar system and travelled beyond contact with Earth. No one knows if its message will ever be received. Travelling at about 25,000 miles per hours away from our sun, scientists tell us that Pioneer 10 will travel towards the general direction of the star Aldebaran (A star in the Constellation Taurus) and would eventually reach that distance in about two million years.

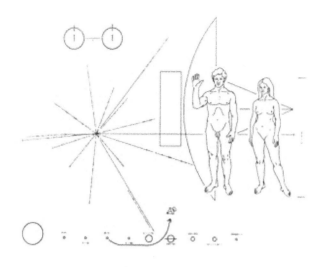

Image on the Pioneer 10 Plaque

There may be many civilizations among the stars and making contact with them is one of humanity's most exciting adventures. But has that contact already been made? Is it possible that astronauts from other worlds have already visited us and left behind their calling cards here on Earth?

We must consider the limitation of time when speculating about alien visitors. If you consider that Pioneer 10 will take 2 million years to reach a star that is extremely close to Earth on the scale of our galaxy; it starts to give us a perspective of time limitation.

Even if a spacecraft could somehow travel at the speed of light: over 670 million miles per hour (about 27,000 times faster than Pioneer 10) the vast distances of the universe would make space travel a very slow process. It would take twenty five thousand years just to get to the nearest galaxy.

Of course we could simply speculate 'hyper-warp travel' like star wars or travelling through 'portals', 'stargates' and 'wormholes'. This science fiction type of travel methods would allow instantaneous travel from one part of the universe to another or perhaps even travel to alternate universes.

But let's leave out these 'star-trek' type solutions for a moment. Let's imagine that we are dealing with physical spacecraft that need to obey all the laws of physics of which we are familiar. Let's say that they probably have anti-gravity technology that allow them to fly faster and maneuver faster than any known military aircraft. But let's suppose they are still physical objects that are subject to time and distance constraints and the occupants are also organic based life forms with some similar basic limitations.

Now, what are the two most common shapes for UFO's? Cigar-shaped and saucer shaped. What are we familiar with from our own technology that is cigar-shaped or saucer shaped?

Cigar-shaped human device

Saucer-shaped human device

Why are these devices shaped like this? So they can withstand pressure from the deep sea. Some deep sea bathyscaphes are also circular shaped as are some UFO's.

When we send spacecraft into space, they are usually not very aerodynamic. Just look at the Apollo Lunar Lander or the International Space station; they do not have to withstand severe pressure or even have a sleek aerodynamic profile. This is what Pioneer 10 looks like:

Pioneer 10

Since it is travelling through empty space, it does not need to deal with crushing pressure. Why don't we see UFO's shaped like this? Why don't UFO's have large awkward landing gear, antennae, exposed struts and so on and so forth?

Could it be because UFO's need to travel underwater? Only a small fraction of the world's oceans have been explored to date. The shape of UFO's themselves could be giving us a clue as to their origins and their travel requirements. Could it be that most UFO's have not come from outer space but have instead come from 'inner space' — under the Earth.

This idea makes more sense than having to travel billions of miles over eons of time. Scientist are discovering new species of animals all the time, who's to say that there could be sub-terrestrials living under the oceans of planet Earth?

Chapter 6 - Unidentified Submerged Objects

Earth has a surface area of over 195 million square miles and over two thirds of it is covered by water. To this day, the vast majority of the seas and oceans remained mostly unexplored. We know more about the secrets and enigmas of the lunar surface than we do about the world's vast seas.

For as long as there have been eyewitness reports about UFO's in the skies, there have also been similar reports about USO's – unidentified submerged objects but these reports have not been as well publicized.

A USO is basically a UFO that goes into and out of the water; in fact you can describe USO's and UFO's as being the same thing; it is simply that a UFO becomes a USO when it submerges.

October 11th, 1492 is documented as one the earliest cases of an eye-witness account of a USO. It actually occurred aboard the Santa Maria, one of the ships of Christopher Columbus. At 10:00 PM on that date it was a calm clear night and Christopher Columbus and his crew were making their way across one of the deepest sections of the Atlantic in the area now known as the Bermuda Triangle. Below them was almost four miles of water (about 20,000 feet depth).

Suddenly un-earthly lights were seen flashing below the surface of the water. One of the crew spotted a disc-shaped object rising out of the water which gave off a brilliant flash of light that startled Columbus and his crew of 120 men aboard the 3-ship fleet. They were just five hours away from their discovery of America.

The log that Columbus kept in his ship describes what could be interpreted as a UFO or USO event. Columbus described it as 'the flickering of a wax candle going up and down in the night'. It could not have been a campfire on land since they were beyond the horizon of the shore. This possible incident is more than just legend, original texts from Columbus' log have been preserved at Fordham University and copies of the hand-written journal have been made available for translation and study.

The October 11th, 1492 sighting was not an isolated event. Over his two month journey Columbus recorded a number of peculiar incidents including unexplained sightings in both the sea and the sky.

***

One of the earliest European sightings was recorded in 1067 in England. People reported seeing a strange object in the sky come down to Earth lighting up the countryside. It descended and then rose up again, when it came back down a second time, it descended into the sea.[5]

***

An even earlier sighting of USO's, what one could consider ancient is from 329 B.C. when Alexander the Great was recorded to have seen shining shield-like objects flying into and out of the

---

[5] Invisible Residents by Ivan T. Sanderson, p. 32

Jaxartes River (now known as the Syr Darya River) in India. This sighting fascinated him to the point that he invested great effort in trying to find them again and also some believe he tried to find the lost realm of Atlantis.

***

The Santa Catalina channel is a twenty-six mile wide stretch of the Pacific Ocean that separates the city of Los Angeles from Catalina Island. According to some, these waters, portions of which might be as deep as Mount Everest is high, may contain mysterious secrets about unidentified submerged objects.

Catalina Island itself has been the site of numerous UFO sightings. In recent years there have been reports of unidentified submerged objects flying into and out of the channel. Some estimate that there have been hundreds of cases of UFO reports in and around the channel. Preston Dennett authored a book entitled, 'UFO's over California' and has been investigating UFO activity in that area for many years.

"There was a huge wave of sightings over the Santa Monica Mountain Range on June 14th, 1992. Witnesses counted a total of about 200 objects. What's interesting about this case is that these objects came from below; normally when someone sees a UFO it comes out of the sky like a star-like object and comes swooping down. These came from below to above." – Preston Dennett

June 14th, 1992 at 10:24 PM for almost two minutes the waters of the Pacific Ocean exploded with light as hundreds of bright disc-like craft were witnessed flying out of the water together. Similar to other reports of USO's these craft emerged in almost complete silence; they hovered for a moment then each burst off into space.

Reports of the above incident were phoned into local police departments as far away as Malibu. The following is an actual transcript from one of those calls:

Deputy: Lost Hills Sheriff's Station

Caller: Did anyone report anything strange tonight?

Deputy: Ahh….can you be a little more specific. Ahh….strange you know…

Caller: Lights.

Deputy: Lights?

Caller: Yes.

Deputy: What exactly happened to you on your way home?

Caller: I'm ashamed to tell you because I think you're gonna think I'm crazy. We saw what we thought was a bright light up in the sky.

Deputy: Okay.

Caller: We could hear it wasn't a helicopter. I'm telling you, I've never been more frightened in my life.

***

According to Dennett, the incident was also reported to the U.S. Coast Guard in Long Beach which ultimately declined to conduct a thorough search. This 1992 event was the second in Los Angeles in three years.

On the dark foggy morning of February 7th, 1989, scuba divers, boat sonar systems and people on the shore witnessed a long dark unidentified craft dive out of the Pacific. For about ninety seconds the USO rested just about the surface before releasing about a dozen smaller fast moving objects. Sixty seconds later, the craft dived back under the water. Its last reported sonar heading was south towards the Santa Catalina Channel before it disappeared.

" ...and it involved dozens of objects that were seen off the coast of Marina Del Ray. On occasion some of these smaller crafts about twenty feet in diameter, were seen under the surface of the ocean, and they would come in and out of the water." – Preston Dennett

As the 1947 incident at Roswell sparked worldwide curiosity about flying saucers, these events near Los Angeles also sparked a wave of research into the capabilities and threats of so called USO's.

The oceans of the world cover 70% of the planet and they hide a lot of mysteries. It is possible that the oceans could be home to sentient creatures because nobody goes there. It is fascinating to think of 'underwater UFO's' because it could be that they know more about our planet than we do.

A remarkable feature of these USO's is that they are commonly reported to multiply and break apart. One such astounding case has become known as the Gulf of Nuevo event. At that time, the Argentinean Navy was on alert as they tracked two underwater submarine-like objects in their territorial waters. They thought they might be American submarines.

Then, according to reports, the underwater objects are seen on sonar to break apart and fly out of the water.

These two large objects were sighted in 1960 and inexplicably multiplied into six other objects. The Argentineans were never able to catch them because they eventually just disappeared. This case even caught the attention of the Soviet Union at the time. Nikita Khrushchev, who was the leader of the Soviet Union at that time, was so intrigued by the whole story that he sent his diplomatic attaché in Buenos Aries to find out what was going on.

While some researchers contend that these reported cases might be nothing more than military submarines firing torpedoes, others argue that submarines were not capable of firing six torpedoes at once in 1960.

Late UFO researcher Ivan T. Sanderson wrote a book in 1970 called 'Invisible Residents'. He is credited with being one of the first to analyze the USO phenomenon.

In his book he reported on another remarkable example of USO behavior. In March of 1963, a U.S. Navy Submarine exercise was progressing as planned one hundred miles off the coast of Puerto Rico. Suddenly one navy sub abruptly broke from its' assigned route after detecting an unidentified object travelling in excess of speeds of 150 knots. The submarine crewmen are astonished at the depth at which the unidentified craft is moving... 20,000 feet below the surface.

This craft was giving off the acoustic signature of a single propeller type of vehicle. A normal submarine would be crushed if it travelled deeper than a depth of 7,000 feet so this thing, whatever it was, exceeded the capabilities of any submarine of that day and even almost all submarine craft of today.

The object was tracked for almost four days by the crew of the U.S. Navy subs and this craft had the capability of scooting away at will, at almost impossible speeds and then stop and rest while the Navy caught up to it.

Reports of this event were sent back to Naval Headquarters in Norfolk Virginia, however an official determination as to what was seen on sonar that day was never made. According to some reports, the Navy lost track of the vessel after midnight of the fourth day of its discovery and was never picked up on sonar again.

Nobody has ever been able to propose a concrete theory as to how something could move that fast. There are reports of USO's moving in and out of the water but there is very little data such as what was recorded in 1963 off the coast of Puerto Rico. UFO's on the other hand are witnessed often whereas USO's remain mostly hidden. If the Navy does have more data on finding USO's, it is unlikely that they would release the information to the general public.

In fact over the years the U.S. Navy has attempted to explain away UFO's as being merely weather balloons.

In spite of denials, reports from around the world have continued. Another extraordinary case was reported in the international press on November 11th, 1972. A fast moving submarine-like object was picked up on sonar in the Sonja Fiord off the west coast of Norway by the Norwegian Navy which hunted it for two weeks. A fleet of surface ships and a number of specially equipped sub-hunter helicopters were engaged to find the object.

On November 20th, 1972 the USO is seen visually for the first time. It was described as being a massive silent cigar-shaped object. One of the Norwegian Navy ships fired upon the craft but it dived away from the attack. The navy then proceeded to fire depth charges without success.

After about two weeks, the navy decided to blockade the fiord in the hopes of trapping the USO. They wanted to seal off the fiord so nothing could get in or out. Nevertheless after 14 or 15 days the USO disappeared prompting many to believe that it could not have been a conventional submarine.

It appears that USO's could have an ability to travel partially under the Earth's crust into layers that to date have been unknown to humans. It has only recently been announced that scientists have discovered evidence of a massive reservoir of water three times the size of Earth's oceans located hundreds of miles underneath the surface of the planet.[6]

If such studies turn out to be correct, it would mean that there is virtually an undiscovered universe under the surface of Earth. This idea is also mentioned a number of times in the Bible. For example in Revelation chapter 5:

"And no man in heaven, nor in earth, neither **under the earth**, was able to open the book, neither to look thereon."

[6] Published in NewScientist.com June 12, 2014 – Andy Coghlan

Some would argue that under the Earth means things that are in the sea but this next passage from Revelation 5 makes a clear distinction between under the Earth and such as are in the sea.

"...every creature which is in heaven, and on the earth, and **under the earth**, and such as are in the sea, and all that are in them..."

The amplified version of the bible describes under the Earth as being the 'place of departed souls' or Hades.

Philippians chapter 2 verse 10 also mention that there are beings under the Earth. Since we are looking at some references from the Bible; that leads us to our next chapter topic.

Chapter 7 - Biblical Records of Aliens

For centuries, scholars have grappled with the question of what UFO's may be, the possible identity of their occupants and where they may have come from. Some of the earliest accounts of UFO's are contained within the pages of the Bible. In spite of containing a number minor contextual errors; - usually related to transcription or translation mistakes- the Bible has had a remarkable record of accuracy with respect to both historical events and prophetic forecasts.

In recent years, the Bible has increasingly been mentioned by investigators as a collection of stories describing encounters with aliens and UFO's. Of course such a position is controversial. Can the traditional interpretation of the biblical texts be challenged?

With the decline of the emphasis on religion by many modern researchers; people are looking for alternative explanations that are more scientific. Instead of believing in creation by God, many people want to explain creation by other alien civilizations from our distant past. There is still a deep desire to know who God is but people are finding different explanations that satisfy their desire for a meaningful and yet palatable history.

The search for humanity's first possible contact with alien beings in prehistoric times leads to this scriptural place; to the Bible's first chapter – the book of Genesis.

Genesis describes conditions in the world at the dawn of time:

"And it came to pass, when men began to multiply on the face of the earth, and daughters were born unto them,

*That the **sons of God** saw the daughters of men that they were fair; and they took them wives of all which they chose...*

*There were **giants in the earth** in those days; and also after that, when the sons of God came in* *unto the daughters of men, and they bare children to them, the same became mighty men which were of old, men of renown."*

Genesis chapter 6 verse 4

Who exactly were these 'giants in the Earth' and the 'sons of God' mentioned in the text? While most English Bibles use the word 'giants', the original Hebrew word is 'Nephilim'. One translation of the word Nephilim is 'men who came down' or 'those who came down', meaning those who came down from the sky. It may not mean necessarily that they were physical giants, it could just be that they were great heroes who came down from the sky and produced a hybrid race.

For many investigators hoping to unlock the mystery of UFO's in the ancient world, the Bible contains other intriguing clues. In fact, depending on the interpretation, one could say the Bible is full of UFO references. One such example would be the story of Moses. 3500 years ago the Bible relates how the Israelites were released from bondage in Egypt. Under the leadership of Moses, the begin a forty year journey through the wilderness on the way to the promised land. But according to the Bible something very mysterious guides the multitude through the barren desert:

And the Lord went before them by day in a pillar of a cloud, to lead them the way; and by night in a pillar of fire, to give them light; to go by day and night:

He took not away the pillar of the cloud by day, nor the pillar of fire by night, from before the people. – Exodus chapter 13 verses 21-22

Some believe that this biblical passage contains another dimension besides the meaning long cherished by Christians and Jews; that is some people believe the pillar of cloud and the pillar of fire would be similar to a cigar-shaped UFO and expresses a theme of an extra-terrestrial intelligence; a form of advanced intelligence that is guiding mankind.

Some of the most intriguing biblical passages concern Mount Sinai and the handing down of the Ten Commandments.

And mount Sinai was altogether on a smoke, because the Lord descended upon it in fire: and the smoke thereof ascended as the smoke of a furnace, and the whole mount quaked greatly.

And when the voice of the trumpet sounded long, and waxed louder and louder, Moses spake, and God answered him by a voice. - Exodus chapter 19 verses 18-19

When Moses returned with the Ten Commandments after his encounter with God on Mount Sinai, his skin mysteriously shined with an unearthly glow, his hair had tuned snow white. This story of Moses has been tied in with an extraterrestrial encounter; some say that his hair may have turned white due to radiation exposure. The notion that the Israelites may have been led to the promised land by some form of extra-terrestrial entity has attracted many adherents in the last few decades but understandably, scientists and religious leaders fiercely challenge this idea.

This is dealing very much with an interpretation and with an issue that is very controversial because if you say that Jehovah is an extra-terrestrial, then that would change the basis of Judaism and Christianity in a very fundamental way.

But it is a question of interpretation; these are things that are easy to speculate. You can look at almost any story from the Bible and find things that could be construed as signs of an extra-terrestrial. However if you want to have such an incredible explanation, you have to have some tangible proof, otherwise these arguments will be seen as mere fantasy and imagining.

Biblical connections to aliens and UFO's are not confined to the book of Exodus. In the second book of Kings, there is the intriguing story of the Prophet Elijah who lived about 900 years before the time of Jesus. While Elijah crosses the Jordan river with Elisha, a strange airborne craft appears:

And it came to pass, as they still went on, and talked, that, behold, there appeared a chariot of fire, and horses of fire, and parted them both asunder; and Elijah went up by a whirlwind into heaven. And Elisha saw it, and he cried, My father, my father, the chariot of Israel, and the horsemen thereof. And he saw him no more... - 2 Kings Chapter 2 verses 11 & 12

A lot of ancient cultures have descriptions of flying chariots that fly through the sky. Many people today feel that these are really descriptions of UFO's.

Just over three centuries after Elijah's ascent into heaven in a chariot of fire, another strange incident occurs. This time it concerns the Hebrew Prophet Ezekial. He is believed by some to have encountered alien spaceships on at least four separate occasions. In one account, he describes a clearly mechanical device under the control of human-like figures.

And when I looked, behold the four wheels by the cherubims, one wheel by one cherub, and another wheel by another cherub: and the appearance of the wheels was as the colour of a beryl stone.

And as for their appearances, they four had one likeness, as if a wheel had been in the midst of a wheel.

And when the cherubims went, the wheels went by them: and when the cherubims lifted up their wings to mount up from the earth, the same wheels also turned not from beside them.

When they stood, these stood; and when they were lifted up, these lifted up themselves also: for the spirit of the living creature was in them.

Then the glory of the Lord departed from off the threshold of the house, and stood over the cherubims.

And the cherubims lifted up their wings, and mounted up from the earth in my sight: when they went out, the wheels also were beside them,

— Ezekial chapter 10 verses 9,10,16 - 19

Based on this biblical description of a strange flying device, in the 1960's NASA engineer Joseph Blumridge constructed a model as in the image below:

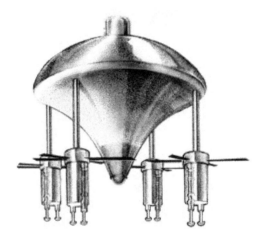

Could this be similar to what Ezekial saw? It could be that Ezekial was experiencing a vision within his own mind or that he was dreaming. Or maybe he simply saw something that he couldn't explain and so he described it as best as he could.

***

There is a startling account in the Bible when Peter receives instructions about reaching out to the gentiles. He is in prayer on the roof of a house when we read:

And (Peter) saw heaven opened, and a certain vessel descending upon him, as it had been a great sheet knit at the four corners, and let down to the earth: - Acts 10 verse 11

Heaven opened and a vessel descending!

If we examine the scripture of Acts 10 verse 11 in the original Greek language, it translates as: "and he beholds the heaven opened and descending upon him a vessel, certain as a sheet great, by four corners bound, and let down upon the Earth"

And again in verse 16 we read:

This was done thrice: and the vessel was received up again into heaven.

Notice in verse 16 it does not say 'the sheet was taken back up', rather "the vessel".

Many read this scripture and simply think Peter had a vision of a sheet coming down from the sky filled with creatures but upon closer examination it actually says that a vessel came down from the sky.

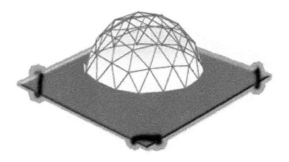

A depiction of the 'vessel' Peter saw.

The above image could be more similar to what Peter saw, with the creatures being contained within the 'dome' portion. Almost all traditional paintings show a literal linen sheet holding creatures. It could be that the writer described it as a sheet because he noticed that the four corners were bound similar to how a sheet could be tied down to a mattress or bed frame.

Just a few verses earlier, Cornelius was visited by an Angel who told him to go and meet Peter, this Angel told him exactly where Peter was staying, his full name and that Peter would have specific news for him.

It seems from this Biblical passage that there is evidence to indicate that some alien vessels are associated with angels.

Many Christians like to speculate that alien beings are demons or demonic in origin. In fact the Bible teaches that demons are severely limited in their ability to interact with and manipulate physical things whereas angels have no such limitation.

Chapter 8 - Angels or Aliens

To expand on the subject of angels and aliens we should start by understanding the difference between them.

According to biblical accounts, angels are beings that have been created by God. They are servants of God and can take on both physical and spiritual form. Psalm 104 tells us that God makes his angels 'spirits'. We are also told that angels can pass for humans without our knowledge as in Hebrews chapter 13 verse 2:

Be not forgetful to entertain strangers: for thereby some have entertained angels unawares.

So it is important to realize that angels are not like fairies or leprechauns; angel cannot dance on the head of a pin; angels are similar to us. They can pass for any human you might see on the street.

We are told in the bible that the devil has his angels. By inference we conclude that Lucifer rebelled against God and took a number of angels with him, presumably those angels voluntarily joined forces with him.

Matthew 25 verse 41 states:

Then shall he say also unto them on the left hand, Depart from me, ye cursed, into everlasting fire, prepared for the devil and his angels...

Isaiah chapter 14 verses 12 to 17 explains about Lucifer which is another name for the devil and was himself an angel also:

How art thou fallen from heaven, O Lucifer, son of the morning! how art thou cut down to the ground, which didst weaken the nations!

For thou hast said in thine heart, I will ascend into heaven, I will exalt my throne above the stars of God: I will sit also upon the mount of the congregation, in the sides of the north:

I will ascend above the heights of the clouds; I will be like the most High.

Yet thou shalt be brought down to hell, to the sides of the pit.

*They that see thee shall narrowly look upon
thee, and consider thee, saying, "Is this the man that
made the earth to tremble, that did shake kingdoms;*

*That made the world as a wilderness, and
destroyed the cities thereof; that opened not the
house of his prisoners?"*

It is interesting to note that Lucifer a.k.a. the
devil, will be seen by onlookers as a man, they ask the
question, "Is this the man?"

So hell, that is the hell we envision when we
think of eternal fire, was actually created for the devil
and his angels not for humans. Lucifer was an angel
himself that for some reason rebelled against God and
was joined by a number of angels.

We are told of a war that either took place in
heaven or will take place in heaven in the future; it is
described in Revelation chapter 12 verses 7 to 9:

*And there was war in heaven: Michael and his
angels fought against the dragon; and the dragon
fought and his angels,*

*And prevailed not; neither was their place found
any more in heaven.*

*And the great dragon was cast out, that old
serpent, called the Devil, and Satan, which deceiveth*

the whole world: he was cast out into the earth, and his angels were cast out with him.

So these angels and the devil are cast out of heaven. We also read in Luke chapter 10 verses 16 to 18:

And the seventy returned again with joy, saying, Lord, even the devils are subject unto us through thy name.

And he said unto them, I beheld Satan as lightning fall from heaven.

So we see that the devil and his angels are expelled from heaven. During Jesus' time on Earth, there were many people who were possessed by 'devils'. For example in Matthew Chapter 8 and verse 16:

When the even was come, they brought unto him many that were possessed with devils: and he cast out the spirits with his word, and healed all that were sick...

These devils are those that have been cast out of heaven and no longer have access to their own physical body. They can only inhabit the body of a human or other living creature by somehow getting access to the inside of them. For example in Matthew 8 verses 30 to 32:

And there was a good way off from them an herd of many swine feeding.

So the devils besought him, saying, If thou cast us out, suffer us to go away into the herd of swine.

And he said unto them, Go. And when they were come out, they went into the herd of swine: and, behold, the whole herd of swine ran violently down a steep place into the sea, and perished in the waters.

So we know now that aliens cannot be devils because devils are spirits. We read in Jude chapter 1 verses 5 to 7:

And the angels which kept not their first estate, but left their own habitation, he hath reserved in everlasting chains under darkness unto the judgment of the great day.

We see that the physical bodies of angels that rebelled and joined themselves to Lucifer are imprisoned. We can infer that Jesus likely bound these angels when he was temporarily dead for three days since this is when he had opportunity to defeat them as is mentioned in Ephesians chapter 4 verses 8 and 9:

Wherefore he saith, When he ascended up on high, he led captivity captive, and gave gifts unto men.

*(Now that he ascended, what is it but that he also descended first into the **lower parts of the earth**?*

So the physical angels that rebelled are called devils and these are imprisoned beneath the Earth somewhere. The spirits of these devils are able to roam the Earth and inhibit living creatures but since their physical bodies are imprisoned, they cannot appear the same way that angels can.

We go through all these details so that we can understand that fallen angels, that is devils, cannot be the same thing as aliens that people have seen piloting UFO's.

Moving on to 'good' angels; these are the angels that serve humanity and carry out the instructions and plans of God. These angels could pilot UFO's if they so desire since they have physical bodies similar to humans. So similar in fact, that if you were to see an angel, you could easily mistake them for a human.

Some people get confused and imagine angels to be twelve feet tall with wings. They are mixing up angels with cherubim. Cherubim are a special type of angel with wings.[7] There are also Seraphim which are also a type of angel but with six wings; three pairs of wings.[8]

Returning to good angels, we have seen earlier that a 'vessel' came down from heaven and appeared to Peter. Even though no angels were seen on the vessel, we are told that an angel went ahead to speak to Cornelius who knew exactly what was happening with Peter.

It appears that good angels have access to technology that they can use for specific purposes when necessary. These vessels likely come up from under the Earth, under the oceans and this would account for many of the UFO sightings that have been witnessed throughout history.

---

[7] For example see Exodus 25 verse 20

[8] For example see Isaiah 6 verse 2

In other words, some UFO's are likely not aliens from outer space, they are aliens from within the Earth. These aliens fly up from under the oceans and then fly through the atmosphere; they have been here all along throughout history but have not been discovered. Angels themselves are a type of advanced beings that were created prior to the creation of humans so they likely have advanced technology at their disposal.

But one would ask, why would angels fly spacecraft? If they have the ability to transform into spirit beings and to disappear at will[9] they really would have no need to fly a mechanical device. Therefore, it is safe to say that we can likely exclude any type of angels as being the pilots of UFO's.

---

[9] For example in Acts chapter 12 verse 10

Chapter 9 - Aliens in the Renaissance

We have seen in Chapter 5 that some ancient artifacts are can have a subjective interpretation when applying them as proof of extra-terrestrials visiting Earth. The farther back in time we search, the more likely that the evidence we find can be interpreted as local cultural expressions or random artistic creations.

Most ancient cultures have snakes or dragons in their art and artifacts. Ancient alien theorists believe these to be representative of extra-terrestrials that visited the Earth in ancient times. Now why do they assume this? First of all we must be aware that ancient cultures were influenced by fallen angels. These fallen angels were on the side of Lucifer who is known as a snake, serpent or dragon. It is obvious that these fallen angels tried to get ancient cultures to join forces with them to pledge allegiance to Satan.

Remember that this was before most of the fallen angels were captured and imprisoned under the Earth; that is why ancient cultures were so heavily influenced by these serpent and dragon representations.

So actually ancient alien theorists are correct in thinking that ancient civilizations were visited by extra-terrestrials, but the extra-terrestrials were actually fallen angels. Ancient alien theorists are unable to see this since they are still under the influence of the fallen angel spirits which are still able to roam the Earth, even though they do not have access to their physical bodies, these fallen angels can still influence thoughts of humans in the spirit realm.

From Revelation chapter 12 we read:

And the great dragon was cast out, that old serpent, called the Devil, and Satan, which deceiveth the whole world: he was cast out into the earth, and his angels were cast out with him.

You can see fours names given here: dragon, serpent, devil and Satan. Also notice that his angels go with him.

Next we read in Isaiah chapter 27 verse 1:

In that day the Lord with his sore and great and strong sword shall punish leviathan the piercing serpent, even leviathan that crooked serpent; and he shall slay the dragon that is in the sea.

Here we see another name for the devil, that is: Leviathan and are given his location as being in the sea.

Let's turn our attention to the period of the Renaissance however; that is the years roughly from about 1350 A.D. to about 1650 A.D. The Renaissance which is a French word which means, 're-birth' or 're-born' was a significant time in history when people allowed themselves, their inner souls, to be influenced by good angels. It is during this time that we see a lot of vivid depiction of UFO's; for example:

This image is from the Palazzo Vecchio in Florence Italy. The painting has been attributed to Jacopo del Sellaio or Sebastiano Mainardi. In the top right corner of the painting is a shepherd looking up at the sky. Here are some close up images:

Here you can see the shepherd is looking up at what appears to be a UFO.

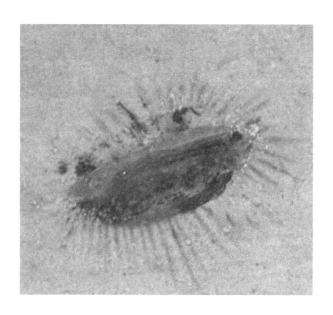

Close up image of UFO or Nativity Star

Some researchers have tried to explain that the painter was merely trying to represent the 'glory of God' or the 'Nativity Star'. And in a sense they are correct; however there is little doubt that this artist was depicting a UFO of alien origin which we will discuss in more detail in the next chapter. Researchers come up with creative ways to dismiss religious depictions of UFO's because they are biased against anything biblical; if the same images were found in cave paintings by primitive civilizations those same researchers would be beside themselves with excitement at such clear proof.

Here is another image from a fresco dated approximately 1350:

Here are close-up images from the top left and top right corners:

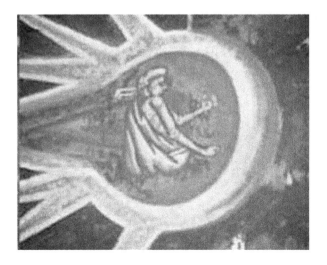

Once again you can see that the artist is depicting UFO's among the stars with occupants. This is not some obscure cave painting nor is it some Mayan creature with a tongue protruding; this is a straight forward image that represents a celestial scene of some type.

Yet another example; this painting is from 1486 and is attributed to Carlo Crivelli. The title of the painting is entitled 'The Annunciation with Saint Emidius':

Here is a close up of the UFO shaped disk that is sending out a beam of light towards Mary:

You can see from the detail of the painting that the artist is showing concentric groups of angels surrounding a beam from heaven or a beam from God. It is clear this artist wanted to portray an event from the heavens in a spiritual way.

There are many more images from the Renaissance that contain images of what appear to be UFO's. This is not surprising since it was a time when humans were being influenced powerfully by angels that were visiting them in spirit form and perhaps also in spacecraft. These angels were able to influence their minds and pass on new knowledge that allowed for the rapid progress of humanity.

Mathematics, language, advanced arts, music, various scientific studies; all these areas blossomed during this time in history and in fact one could argue that the level of genius that cropped up at that time has never since been equaled on such a massive scale.

Chapter 10 - The Star of Bethlehem

In the last chapter we talked about the 'nativity star' or the UFO that was depicted in the painting from the Palazzo Vecchio in Florence Italy. Here is that image once again:

Now let's examine another painting entitled, 'The Baptism of Christ' which was painted in 1710 by the Flemish artist Aert De Gelder:

In this painting we can see that the artist has painted a disk in the sky that is shining down beams of light. This is a good representation of what the star of Bethlehem could have looked like and now you will understand why. Even though this work of art was painted to represent the baptism of Jesus, it would also be a good depiction of the 'nativity', the traditional scene where Jesus was born.

Let me start by saying that I have seen multiple documentaries that have tried to come up with an explanation as to what the star of Bethlehem may have been. One was by the History Channel, an American Cable Channel owned by Walt Disney, the other by Rick Larsen, a lawyer and independent researcher.

For the most part these studies claim that the star of Bethlehem was an alignment of stars and/or planets that occurred at that particular time in history. They calculate the time of these planetary alignments sometime after 1 B.C., the time of the death of King Herod. In general these studies are thorough and well documented; in particular Larsen's results are quite compelling. However in spite of their well thought out ideas, they miss a fundamental fact about the Star of Bethlehem.

Let's look at Matthew chapter 2 verses 1 to 13:

Now when Jesus was born in Bethlehem of Judaea in the days of Herod the king, behold, there came wise men from the east to Jerusalem,

Saying, Where is he that is born King of the Jews? for we have seen his star in the east, and are come to worship him.

When Herod the king had heard these things, he was troubled, and all Jerusalem with him.

And when he had gathered all the chief priests and scribes of the people together, he demanded of them where Christ should be born.

And they said unto him, In Bethlehem of Judaea: for thus it is written by the prophet,

And thou Bethlehem, in the land of Juda, art not the least among the princes of Juda: for out of thee shall come a Governor, that shall rule my people Israel.

Then Herod, when he had privily called the wise men, enquired of them diligently what time the star appeared.

And he sent them to Bethlehem, and said, Go and search diligently for the young child; and when ye have found him, bring me word again, that I may come and worship him also.

*When they had heard the king, they departed; and, lo, **the star, which they saw in the east, went before them, till it came and stood over where the young child was.***

When they saw the star, they rejoiced with exceeding great joy.

And when they were come into the house, they saw the young child with Mary his mother, and fell down, and worshipped him: and when they had opened their treasures, they presented unto him gifts; gold, and frankincense and myrrh.

And being warned of God in a dream that they should not return to Herod, they departed into their own country another way.

*And when they were departed, behold, **the angel of the Lord appeareth to Joseph in a dream**, saying, Arise, and take the young child and his mother, and flee into Egypt, and be thou there until I bring thee word: for Herod will seek the young child to destroy him.*

I have highlighted in bold two key statements from the above biblical passage. The first is "the star, which they saw in the east, went before them, till it came and stood over where the young child was."

93

Now it should be blatantly obvious that a conjunction of Jupiter and Venus cannot come and stand over a spot on the Earth. In fact, by inference from verse 11, it stood over the house where Jesus was.

An observer on Earth may be guided by a bright star, for example to follow the North Star, sailors could follow a specific direction on the compass, like North or East or West or South. The Magi could have followed a specific star or a conjunction of stars/planets to get to Jerusalem. After they reached Jerusalem, they could not get any more indication of where to go from the star. Otherwise, why would they stop and ask for directions?

Herod told them to go to Bethlehem, a short distance from Jerusalem and then they saw the star again but this time the 'star' did not lead them in a general direction, it came down and stood over a specific spot.

Look at any star in the night sky and try and tell me that it can guide someone to a specific house – that is simply not going to happen. If Jupiter or Venus or a specific star came down to Earth, it would wipe out the Earth – that is simply a nonsensical explanation. To repeat, to try and follow a specific star in the sky, you may be able to go in a very general direction but it simply cannot point out a specific location on the Earth – it's not rocket science, it's simple logic.

After the Magi left Jerusalem, they saw a 'star' that was able to guide them as if it was flying above the treetops in the distance. It was quite simply a UFO. Matthew thought it was a miraculous thing that it was the same star that they saw in the East; even he is amazed as he is relating what happened. The Magi are ecstatic at seeing the star – yet it is clear that they lost sight of the first star that led them to Jerusalem and that this is a second 'star' – a 'star' that is able to hover above land that a traveler can actually follow on foot along a specific path, along a specific street, and eventually to a specific house - a UFO if there ever was one.

Secondly notice that an angel appears to Joseph in a dream right after the Magi leave. This was obviously the angel that was piloting the UFO that guided the Magi from Jerusalem to Bethlehem. The original star that guided them from the west (probably Babylon) to Jerusalem could have very well been the conjunction of stars and planets as discussed in the popular documentaries mentioned earlier. It seems that the past positions of the stars lines up quite precisely with dates and events at the time of the birth of Jesus – however, the second 'star' as described in Matthew chapter 2 verse 9 cannot logically have been able to hover above a specific house location allowing the Magi to find the young Jesus in a residence with his parents.

In spite of this glaringly obvious conclusion, if you ask most people with Christian faith, they will simply say that the star came and appeared above where Jesus was. They would rather cling to their illogical belief than be forced to accept the reality of what must have actually occurred.

I am not trying to say that all UFO's are piloted or guided by angels; this is only one instance in history. They are likely many different types of UFO and as we grow in understanding, we will no doubt find many more varieties of extra-terrestrials and how they fit in to the grand plan of the cosmos.

Chapter 11 - Grey Aliens

Our topic of ancient aliens has taken us from ancient artifacts to underwater UFO to angels and demons; but what about the 'traditional' alien creature with which we are so familiar; the prototypical 'grey alien'.

This is the type of aliens that were supposedly found at Roswell and also responsible for the famous abductions of Betty and Barney Hill.[10] Is there any evidence of grey aliens from the ancient past?

Here are a couple of images described as the Predionica Mask from prehistoric times found in the region of modern day Kosovo.

---

[10] See Alien Abduction by Sean Keyhoe for an analysis & effective debunking of the Betty and Barney Hill case:

http://www.amazon.com/dp/B00GPYEV9G

Apparently this mask is in the Kosovo Metohija Regional Museum and is associated with ancient Ninca culture. One researcher[11] suspected that this mask was an inspiration for Ted Jacob's who did the cover of Whitley Striber's very popular book, Communion.

---

[11] David Halpern, http://www.davidhalperin.net/

Cover of book 'Communion'

But what if Ted Jacob's never saw this ancient artifact? If so, then this would again be another excellent example of the depiction of an alien creature in ancient society.

If we look at the typical large almond shaped eyes of the grey alien we could speculate that these are needed due to a lack of light in their normal surroundings. If these aliens resided under the Earth, it would make sense that they need larger eyes. Here is a screen capture of a grey alien from a video that was anonymously posted to the internet in 2011.

Grey Alien

You can see a copy of this video with commentary at the following link:

http://youtu.be/A4dVcnik94M

This video has commentary from an individual who is familiar with CGI (computer generated imagery) and animatronics. He gives a compelling case for the genuineness of the footage. In case you are unable to access the video, I include the transcript below:

"I decided to do a commentary on this particular footage here. Right here, I want you to take a look at this amazing footage. Now in my career of looking at this type of footage in the last twenty years, I have never seen footage of an alien that I deemed real or even suspected of being real. But this I deem absolutely real. I mean look at the way the eye blinks, I mean look at this close up footage. The facial structure and the movement, it doesn't just stretch like skin, it also moves in a fluent motion unlike CGI. An what you have to understand about that is the only way to duplicate this type of fluent motion in CGI is to put, you've probably seen an example of someone in a studio in a black suit with these little dots on their knuckles and so on. You would have to have the dots on the eyelids of something like this to track the movement otherwise it would basically be robotic like movement because you would have programmed it.

This is completely, every bit of it is fluent motion and that tells me that what we're looking at is footage. I mean I can absolutely tell you what we're looking at here is not CGI. I mean if you look across the forehead there's way too much three dimensional characteristics here of what we're actually looking at footage film of a three dimensional; I mean character. There's no way around what we're looking at here.

And on top of that, to think that this is some kind of magnificent suit, or anatomic doll is absolutely unbelievable. Look here, we got the hands like; look at, they move; I mean look how long the thumb is. And again, this is footage; you can see the texture of the wall behind, you can see the three dimensions. I mean everything; look at the shadowing. Look at the shadowing, I mean, that's another thing; every single shadow and line and lighting is just perfect.

I have not seen CGI to this day that doesn't have to hide the camera; you know what I mean. Even look at today's most modern fake alien videos on YouTube and you'll see when they use CGI to fake an alien, they only turn the camera on it for a couple of seconds at best so that you can't sit down and analyze it. Right here we have a fully frontal view. No attempt to try and hide or disguise anything.

The only attempt that I can find to try and disguise anything is the black and white seems to be a program; seems to be that they took the color away and made it black and white. Maybe to disguise, maybe they didn't want us to know when. Obviously somebody controlling and leaking this kind of information. See this stain on the wall in the background? I mean, come on; look at the three dimensions here around the head. This is fully frontal three dimensional, look at the face, this thing is magnificent. The skin, the focus, that's the biggest thing that lets you know that this isn't CGI.

If I wanted to pull off a fake alien in CGI like this, I would blur it. Motion blur it so that you can't see that it's CGI because right here we can clearly see that this is real; this is real.

Now of course, somebody who doesn't know anything about CGI would say, "Oh, that can be CGI." It's not, no it can't be CGI. You can't take a frame from Avatar and make it black and white and make it look like it's real footage. You know, the movements aren't right; it doesn't work that way. You know, you can watch Avatar black and white all day long and you're still going to be able to pick out what's real and what's phony.

You know, CGI has not gotten to the point where it will fool someone into thinking it is completely realistic; if it had, our video games would be almost total virtual reality and they're not. You know, I play the best video games sometimes and you know they're great but there's still that digital look; you can still kinda see that cartoony look with the best attempts. Even when they copy a real image of someone and make it digital, it still doesn't look like a real image of someone and making it black and white and blurring it isn't going to do that.

That's evident by the other video of the blurry alien supposedly caught in Brazil. You know that didn't fool anyone, that was ridiculous. But the thing is, I'm gonna say that this is real and I'm a fan of the show 'Face-Off'. Anyone familiar with Face-Off knows that those guys are really elite costume anatomic builders and they do this kind of stuff. But if you look, there's no stretchy, eyelid blinking, holy shit, come on people, look at this thing.

Screen capture from video of Grey Alien

I want you to take a look at something over here. By the neck, right under where you think the ear would be, there's this little shape there, almost maybe would look like the vein or your tendon. I want you to pay special close attention to just that general area as he turns his head, flexes and I want you to look at how the skin and the shadowing stretches and moves slightly.

To do this in CGI, this would be the most magnificent piece of CGI known to man right now because this piece of CGI would be the first in history to actually be so realistic that it could fool somebody into thinking that this is real. If this is CGI I am fooled and this would be the first time I would be glad to have a video game made out of this because I could feel like I was in the game and I would think why make it black and white? I could put color, I probably will end up putting color into this thing just to show you that color – they'd be no reason to make it black and white.

I want you to pay attention to areas like this as this thing moves, look at you know, if you look close enough, you will realize you are actually looking at a three dimensional object not a two dimensional object trying to fool you into an illusion. When you draw a three dimensional box on a chalkboard, it's not really three dimensional, it's flat. You just draw it that way and that's pretty similar to making a 3-D image on a computer. It's not really a 3-D image, there's no skin stretching over so you know, in order for that to happen, you have to do programming for each and every individual area where the shadowing has skin stretching over it and that's what I'm saying.

You look at areas like how the skin, how the shadowing moves across it, all those little details and that's why I've zoomed in on some of this so that we can have some details here and look at some of these points that I'm bringing up about this footage. Basically there is no debate, there is no debate: this is footage.

So, if you want to debate this, you're going to have to try to claim that this is some kind of mask and you're going to have to come with something like, so and so made a mask that does this; you're going to have to explain why every attempt to make a fake alien video does not hold a candle to this right here.

This is what I believe part of the 'soft' disclosure that's been taking place in the last three or four years. This came out in 2011 I believe, right before 2012 and I could be wrong. I think this could have come out in 2012. I tell you what; somebody covered up some things like made it black and white. That flash is timed so you can tell it's software made to duplicate black and white. So they wanted you to think that this footage was older than it really is.

It could be somebody leaked it trying to hide their tracks. There could be a variety of reasons why they would make it black and white to cover the age of it. But that's the thing, at least we know that black and white is an awesome way to cover the age. And it would, it weren't for that one little slip of color in it.

So I think we're seeing the first footage of an alien and it makes sense to me because we have the skeletons anyway. The bottom line is, these people that won't believe this simply because of the subject matter are being very narrow minded from the fact that we have bodies of these beings with DNA that says they are non-terrestrial; not linked to any primate; however their mitochondrial DNA was human. Obviously meaning they abducted females nine hundred years ago and impregnated them with their own kind.

The bottom line, it proves two things happened nine hundred years ago. One, there was genetic manipulation going on. And two there were greys about four feet tall with big heads and big eyes who abducted human females to carry their offspring. That was reported in the last century, thousands and thousands of people reported that very thing and sure enough we find skeletons.

Now, we have this footage that looks real and everybody's trying to say, "Well it can't possibly be real." Why not? Obviously these things have been flying around. Obviously at Roswell they did crash; people saw them. So obviously there is footage of these things.

This particular footage I think is quite amazing. I think what's going on in this picture, is you're seeing the alien sitting at a table solving a jigsaw puzzle. You know, like they would do a monkey. Sit a monkey down and hand it a box with a clover and triangle shaped block and they put it in the hole. He moves it, he looks down at the table, moves his arms, he looks up, he looks back down and then he looks up and he smiles. It looks to me like he's solving a puzzle really quick and then he's looking back up at the people and smiling.

And then the next shot is even more amazing, a fully frontal profile. This is obviously like a mug shot except using footage. This is exactly what I would expect the military to take as far as documentation of what a being looks like. This is incredible footage, this is not a hoax; this is a very serious piece of disclosure and I think ufology needs to take this very seriously.

And people need to quit saying, 'this is CGI' without the credentials to say that is CGI. You know, unless you can make this, then don't say it's CGI. And I can't make it.

Now I'll tell you, maybe Avatar is beautiful and everything but you're not going to be able to put black and white on Avatar and make me think that one piece of that is real. If you can, good luck. I have never once thought any CGI UFO or CGI alien was real, ever...never. Before I deemed even a UFO photo real, it's got to have validated reports on MUFON the reporting center, eyewitnesses. You know, the kind of research that I do, I'm going down to the volcano in Mexico that frequents UFO's on their government camera to see if there's eyewitnesses to support these footage sightings.

So I don't just 'believe' in the stuff, I like to know things and I have enough experience in CGI to know that this footage is not CGI at all. The blinks are not CGI. The muscle tone and the skin stretching over that muscle is not CGI, this is real footage and I can kind of tell what's going on there. Of course they have the alien sat down at a desk, he solves a puzzle, looks up like a smart ass and smiles at the guy and the other they're showing the fully frontal.

Obviously the alien submitted to the fully frontal documentary footage so they can disclose this to people. Not to people like you and I but probably people in charge of shit. Anyway, this needs to be real popular. People need to start seeing this for what it is and other people that don't have the right credentials need to stop commenting that this is CGI. And other people who aren't fans of the show 'Face-Off', that don't know shit about the best Hollywood mask-making techniques, need to quite saying this could be anatomics because look at what they can do today. They can't do this shit, sorry."

I am not sure exactly what evidence this commentator is referring to when he mentions skeletons and 900 year old genetic manipulation but he seems to make a persuasive argument for the genuineness of the grey alien video. It would interesting to see if a special effects costume expert could come forward and replicate the type of alien seen in this video.

One may wonder whether the 'grey' type of alien was formed from actual contact experiences or from the imagination of humanity. When we think of a vampire, we think of fangs and a widow-peak haircut ; when we think of Frankenstein, we think of bolts in the neck, a square head and a large body. In a similar way, the prototypical 'grey' alien has become a part of culture with the grey skin, almond shaped eyes and short stature.

It would come as a relief to finally find definitive proof of their existence, as might be found in the above video or something similar or perhaps something even more definitive.

Chapter 12 - Concluding Thoughts

While many believe that the Earth has been visited by extra-terrestrials and their spacecraft, could this indeed be possible? Reports of strange unidentified flying objects have continuously trickled in throughout the centuries echoing incidents from ancient times. By the 1940's, the term 'flying saucer' had become a part of the vocabulary of a fascinated world. Suddenly, seemingly everywhere, the skies were filled with UFO's of every description. In the ensuing decades, UFO's were witnessed by persons of all levels of society; even astronauts saw them.

"I personally believe in UFO's and I believed in UFO's before I got into the space program. I just personally believe that there are other civilizations somewhere out there; that people are travelling from.

It was in the early 1950's when I was flying fighters in Germany and these objects were coming over our base that appeared to be the same kind of formations that we fly in our fighters. On occasion, their movements were more erratic than ours which meant they could really move; accelerate laterally and accelerate fore and aft more readily than we did. We felt they look very much like high flying fighters except they had no wings.

They were certainly higher and faster than anything of the airplanes we know of here on Earth at that particular time. And they certainly appeared to be saucer shaped and metallic."

- Colonel Gordon Cooper

Why are UFO's so seemingly secretive and elusive? If extra-terrestrials are visiting the Earth, some people believe this question can only be answered by direct face-to-face contact with them. In 1977 NASA sent two robotic Voyager spacecraft on an ambitious exploratory tour to Jupiter, Saturn, Uranus and Neptune, the four giant outer planets. Their epic journey took twelve years to complete but they acquired more scientific data about our solar system than had been learned in the previous five hundred years. Perhaps this is the UFO's mission to planet Earth; to explore our world on behalf of another technologically advanced civilization somewhere in the far-flung reaches of the cosmos.

We now know that the chances of finding intelligent life in our own solar system are extremely unlikely. Our sun is but one of billions in our galaxy. And the Milky Way Galaxy, our galaxy, is but one of billions of galaxies spread throughout the universe. Facing these odds is it likely that we are alone? In August 1996, scientists announced that life might have once existed on Mars. Just a few months earlier, the first planet orbiting another sun was confirmed to be 8 light years or a staggering 50 trillion miles from Earth, on a cosmic scale, that is literally just down the road from our own backyard. Today we know a lot about the universe and that there is a real possibility that there could be life out there but most of what you hear about it is nonsense. This is because people are willing to accept the most bizarre stories without proof and there are many stories from all over the world of people seeing strange lights in the sky. Some of these stories are true, there are strange lights in the sky but they usually have an explanation.

There are all kinds of things going on around us and the average person doesn't know about this so they see something weird and they say, "Wow, that must be of extra-terrestrial origin." So there is a tremendous amount of gullibility all over the world.

I believe that the most compelling evidence point to some UFO's as being of extra-terrestrial origin but also that some UFO's have been on Earth since ancient times. These terrestrial UFO's are sometimes accessing a location under the oceans and that it is possible that some of these UFO's are often directed by angels and piloted by grey aliens.

We live on a planet revolving around a star in the middle of an unknown infinity of space. Isn't it strange to imagine that we are the only life in this enormous universe? If you take our ancient texts seriously they all tell us that the universe was created as a home for life; that the universe if full of life. For some it is obvious that there are many other intelligent life forms in the universe. For these people, it would highly plausible that these life forms have visited Earth in the past, do so in the present and will continue to do so in the future.

~ Sean Keyhoe

BONUS Chapter

From the book: 'Alien Abduction' by Sean Keyhoe

Now we come to a case that is not as well known to the general public; a movie was never made about it; the participants did not seek any fame or fortune from their experience and yet it stands as one of the most startling cases of Alien Abduction ever recorded.

This incident occurred on the banks of the Pascagoula River on October 11th, 1973. Charles Hickson and Calvin Parker were planning on an evening of fishing but landed something beyond their wildest expectations. This interview was conducted in 1987:

Charles Hickson and Calvin Parker

Charles Hickson: "I don't think I'll ever forget what did happen, of course it was on October 11th of '73. I was employed by FB Walter & Son Shipyard at that time, Calvin was also, a friend of mine. Many evenings after work, I'd go fishing on the river when I'd have time so that day in particular at noon, Calvin and myself had planned on going fishing that evening after work.

After we, we had gone home and got our tackle of course, we went down to the river; we tried several places and we came back up to the old shipyard and I don't know whether…,what really attracted my attention but I heard a hissing like sound and when I turned and looked behind me there was something, some kind of craft. It was probably eighteen inches or a foot off the ground just hovering there. And there were two blue lights towards the front of it and they were either revolving or pulsing. And I really didn't know what to think; I didn't know what it was, it startled me at first. I stepped down off of the pier and looked around, I saw Calvin stepped down too, he was doing the same thing I was; and about the time we stepped on the ground, there was a door opened there in the front, it just seemed to appear there, probably a sliding door.

There was a brilliant light that came out, from outside of the craft, just a beam of light. And there

---

[12] A quote from Hickson: "After thinking more about it, I believe they were more like robots. They acted like they had a specific thing to do and they did it."

was something that, well I know now it was robots[12], but there was something that came into the door, there was three of them in fact, one behind the other one and they just seemed to glide out of the door; and they never touched the ground. I didn't know what to do, I'm quite frightened at that time; and the river's behind us, we couldn't go that way, so, and those things was getting close to us.

When they got up real close to me I guess I just froze, I don't know, then they came around and one of them took hold of this arm and I felt pain in it just instantly and one of them took hold of the other arm. I seemed to just rise up from the ground at the height they were in more or less a leaning position.

They weren't very tall, I mean I'm five foot eight and I was a little taller than they were. And about that time, Calvin, he was to my right. I saw one take hold of him and he just went limp. And I found out later that he had passed out, he fainted from the fear I suppose. Anyway these things, we just went right on in to the craft through that door and that bright light; went in to probably was the middle of a room or compartment; it appeared to me it was round and the light was glowing from the walls and overhead and the floor.

We stopped about mid-ways in the room I suppose and they just released me. I couldn't move anything but my eyes, I could move my eyes, don't know why I could move them but not anything else. But anyway they released me and a few moments I suppose it was, but out directly in front of me something came out of the wall that appeared to me just a big, I always referred to it as an eye, a big pupil and eye. And it moved up in front of my face and remained there for a few moments, minutes I suppose and it went down and went under me and I'm assuming it went up the backside cuz it came back up over my head, came back in front of me and it remained there for a few more, probably a minute or two or more. And it moved back into the light in the wall and disappeared."

I was still suspended there, I didn't know, there wasn't anything I could do, I just kept wondering what are they gonna do with me? Are they gonna take me away or; I couldn't imagine what they were gonna do or what they were doing with me. But anyhow after a while these things came back and they took hold of me and we seemed to turn in the room and we moved back out of the doorway and they moved back almost to the exact spot that they had picked me up from and they just released me and I fell to the ground.

Well it was thing time that I saw Calvin again and he was, he was standing there in front of the river with his arms outstretched and he appeared to me to be going in shock. I was trying to get up on my feet to make it to him to see if I could help him some way and I heard that hissing sound again and I looked behind me and I saw those blue lights just instantly and this craft it just went away.

Well I made my way on to Calvin and I could get up on my feet by this time and it took me a while to get him where I could talk to him and assure him that maybe, you know, we weren't hurt bad I know but we really didn't know what they had done to us.

At first we decided we wouldn't tell anyone, we'd just keep it to ourselves because, you know, I didn't want to be called a nut and crazy; those things are just not supposed to happen. But the more I thought about it, the more I realized that we had to tell someone maybe the military because, you know possibly our country could be a threat to our country.

So we stopped on the way home, I called Keesler Air Force Base from a pay phone and briefly I tried to explain to them what had happened but they informed me that they didn't handle those things, that we'd have to go through the local sheriff's department.

Well we hesitated there, we didn't want to go through the sheriff's department because, you know, they might just grab us up and take us on to the nut house. But anyway we talked it over again and decided we would call the sheriff's department and maybe we could get them to assure us that we wouldn't have any publicity about it.

So I called the sheriff's department and they sent two deputies over which after talking with us asked us to follow them to the sheriff's department and we did. And they questioned us there for several hours and the sheriff assured me that night that we wouldn't have any publicity about it at all, he would maybe try to report it to the proper authorities; whoever the proper authorities were it could be investigated.

But the next day when we reached work my telephone was ringing and it was some reporter from Jackson and then all the telephones at the shipyard started ringing. They were trying to get information about what happened to Charlie Hickson and Calvin Parker that past night in Pascagoula.

As a whole, I think the public has been real decent to me. I haven't had any ridicule over all these years; I think that's because I've been honest and when people wanted to ask me questions about it, I took up my time to do it.

Sometimes I think maybe I shouldn't have told anyone what happened to me on the Pascagoula river many years ago, but then again I realize that I did right by telling what happened. I think most of the people knows where man has been. I think I know where we are going; maybe someday I can help convince the world of that fact. I know there's other worlds out there with life on it and someday everyone will know that to be a fact without any doubt

In later life, Charles Hickson made these comments:

"There has to be a world out there somewhere, I don't know where it is, there has to be a world out there somewhere they come from.

     ***

Although not as well known as the Betty and Barney Hill case or the Travis Walton Case, this incident was also attacked by Philip Klass. Both men passed a polygraph but Philip Klass claimed the examiner was inexperienced. Others have brought up concerns that Calvin Parker changed his story in later years; that he eventually claimed he had not really passed out but had strange experiences on board the craft.

Charles Hickson passed away in 2011 at the age of 80. He never changed his story. In spite of detractors and the negative comments from skeptics, the Pascagoula Incident is one of the most compelling cases I have found in the area of Alien Abduction.

The day of the incident Hickson and Parker were interviewed by the local Sheriff and they played a kind of sneaky trick on the two men. They leave them alone by themselves at the police station in a room that had a hidden tape recorder. They figured that they would quickly know if they were cooking up a hoax by listening in on their private comments. The recording revealed that the men were in a genuine state of distress and shock at what they had just excperienced. Here is a partial transcript from that secret recording:

Calvin Parker: I almost had a heart attack and I ain't shitting you, I came one damn inch from dying.

Charlie Hickson: I know it scared me to death too. Jesus...have mercy.

Calvin Parker: I was standing there crying like, I just couldn't help it. What's so bad, nobody will believe us.

Charlie Hickson: I know it, I couldn't take much more of that. I thought I'd been through enough hell on this Earth, now I had to go through this.

Calvin: I tell you I need to get some pills or go see a doctor or something, I can't stand it, I'm about to go all crazy.

CHARLIE: I tell you, when we're through, I'll get you something to settle you down so you can get some damn sleep.

CALVIN: I can't sleep yet like it is. I'm just damn near crazy.

CHARLIE: Well, Calvin, when they brought you out-when they brought me out of that thing, goddamn it I like to never in hell got you straightened out.

CALVIN: My damn arms, my arms, I remember they just froze up and I couldn't move. Just like I stepped on a damn rattlesnake.

CHARLIE: They didn't do me that way.

CALVIN: I passed out. I expect I never passed out in my whole life.

CHARLIE: I've never seen nothing like that before in my life. You can't make people believe.

CALVIN: I don't want to keep sitting here. I want to see a doctor.

CHARLIE: They better wake up and start believing... they better start believing.

CALVIN: You see how that damn door come right up?

CHARLIE: I don't know how it opened, son. I don't know.

CALVIN: It just laid up and just like that those son' bitches-just like that they come out.

CHARLIE: I know. You can't believe it. You can't make people believe it-

CALVIN: I paralyzed right then. I couldn't move.

CHARLIE: They won't believe it. They gonna believe it one of these days. Might be too late. I knew all along they was people from other worlds up there. I knew all along. I never thought it would happen to me.

CALVIN: You know yourself I don't drink

CHARLIE: I know that, son. When I get to the house I'm gonna get me another drink, make me sleep. Look, what we sitting around for. I gotta go tell Blanche... what we waiting for?

CALVIN: I gotta go to the house. I'm getting sick. I gotta get out of here.

CALVIN: It's hard to believe . . . Oh God, it's awful... I know there's a God up there.

The day after the incident, Hickson and Parker were interviewed by the military at Keesler Air Force Base at which time it was revealed that others had also witnessed a UFO at the same corroborating their story including a Parole Officer by the name of Raymond Broadus.

A MUFO journal from 1984 published a report on the military interview that is included below. The military did not want to release this transcript and it interesting to see how it corroborates their testimony with the eyewitness accounts from a local parole office and a gas station attendant.

Charlie Hickson always said he thought he remained conscious throughout the experience but he also admitted that he might have lost consciousness since he didn't exactly remember leaving the craft; it was more like he just found himself back outside again. The Pascagoula Incident remains as one the more compelling cases of Alien Abduction to this day.

1984 MUFON Report on Pascagoula Incident

On October 12,1973, the day after Charles Hickson and Calvin Parker reported being taken aboard a UFO while fishing in Pascagoula, Mississippi, they were taken to Keesler Air Force Base in nearby Biloxi to be interviewed by Air Force officials. The transcript of that interview has never been released, although Air Force officials had promised to send a copy to the sheriff of Jackson County while refusing to give Hickson or his attorney, Joe Colingo, a copy.

Now a copy of that transcript has surfaced, being given to MUFON by Ran Stanford, of Austin, Texas. Stanford said he received a copy of the transcript from the father of one of the Air Force officers who took part in the interview.

Following are major portions of the transcript, which was edited down because of its length.

12 October 1973

The following is a transcription of a report made this date by the following individuals:

Mr. Charles Hickson , Mr. Calvin Parker, Jr.,

The report was made to the following personnel:

Lt. Colonel Derrington, Security Police.

Colonel Amdall, Chairman, Department of Medicine.

Colonel Rudolph, Hospital Service.

Colonel Hanson, Veterinary Services

Lt. Colonel Gibson, Associate Administrator.

Major Winans, Health Physicist.

Captain Hoban, Security Police.

MSgt. Russell, Security Police.

T.E. Huntley, Detective, Jackson County Sheriff's Office,

J o e Colingo , Attorney ,Pascagoula,

Mr. Hickson and Mr. Parker both stated they were employed in Pascagoula by F.B. Walker & Sons,

Two persons who reported sighting an object at approximately the same time were: Raymond Broadus, Probation and Parole Officer, Pascagoula. Larry, Larry's Standard Station, Market & Highway 90, Pascagoula.

Lt. Colonel Derrington: I think the best way is to let them tell it as they recall it and then, on specifics, let them fill in areas for clarification.

Charles Hickson: Yesterday evening— I work at the shipyard and when I come in we decided we would go fishing. And the tide wasn't right and we didn't go out in a boat or anything, we thought we would go down — I don't know whether you are familiar with that area or not where the grain elevator is— on the west bank of the river where the shipyard is. So we fished a while there and didn't have any luck and I told Calvin, who was with me, that we'd goon up the river a little further toward the shipyard. I had fished that area in there and loved fishing in there. We hadn't been there very long — we sat on the bank with our spinning reels — when all of a sudden there was a noise. Well what I just heard was a buzzing. I don't know why I turned around. I guess it was to see what it was. It was a blue light— a real light, bright blue light. It could have been purple or something like that. I mean, I would say it was blue at the time I seen the light. At the time I seen the light it just seemed to stop. I would say it was approximately 25 to 30feet away from us, and I didn't know what to think. I was real frightened. I was scared and I know he (Calvin Parker) was from the appearance he had. It seemed that it didn't have exactly a door. It seemed that one end of it just opened up. Three things came out of it — and they didn't touch the ground — just floating, you know, slowly, a couple of feet off the ground. And I couldn't believe it. I was just —

Derrington: You say three things came out of it. What did these three things appear?

Hickson: At the distance I couldn't tell. I mean, it was just immediately where we were.

Derrington: How large was the item hovering?

Hickson: It wasn't round. It seemed oval shaped and it was approximately 8ft. wide, it was a little longer than that, and it had to be over 8 ft. high. When they approached us — one on each side of my arms — but I didn't feel any sensation at all when it touched me. And amazingly I was just lifted right off the ground.

Derrington: You were lifted right off the ground?

Hickson: I was so scared I didn't pay too much attention to what they were doing to him — that was with him. And they carried me through the — I don't know what it was — and as we were in this thing — anything in there that I know of — if I did I didn't have any sensation of touching anything. The whole room like thing seemed to glow. I didn't see anything like light fixtures —just a glowing inside. There were no chairs or anything that I seen. And I didn't see any instruments, although I seen things that I just can't explain what it was. There was things in there.

Derrington: What time of day was this?

Hickson: It was at night.

Derrington: What time?

Hickson: Well, I don't exactly know what time it was because I don't have a watch. It was quite a while after dark.

Derrington: Quite a while after dark?

Hickson: Yes. I don't know — it resembled an eye — but it was a big thing like a globe — but it just moved all around me.

Derrington: This thing, or individual that came after you, you don't have any feel for what it was?

Hickson: Yes, sir. It had features of a human being, but it didn't have any hands. It had pinchers, or something like that.

Derrington: Could you tell if it looked more mechanical than human?

Hickson: No. I just don't know if it looked mechanical more than human. They were real pale looking to me. And I do remember specifically that on what I thought was their feet, there were no toes or anything like that. It was just almost round. It just seemed like it might have been just skin tight what they had on. But I didn't see any clothes. I don't know if I was so frightened, but I didn't see any kind of hair or anything on them. One of them made just some sort of sound. It is hard to say what kind of sound he did make, but the other two — I never heard one sound. Inside the vehicle I did not hear any sound.

Derrington: You mentioned earlier the sound when this thing approached.

Hickson: A buzzing sound. Calvin Parker: Turned around and it was there.

Detective Huntley: You, said there were eyes, a mouth, and a nose.

Hickson: Yes, I don't know whether you would call it a nose. ,It was something sitting on a body and

144

a sharp thing come out about middle ways of the eyes and it looked like an opening to me underneath, and things on the side like ears, I don't know.

Parker: When they got me and took me toward the ship I passed out but it just looked like a ghost out there. It was like if something came through that wall there. .

Hickson: I don't think I could have possibly lost consciousness while I was inside of it. I don't think I did. I think I was conscious all the time.

Derrington: How long were you onboard?

Hickson: I don't know how long we were on board. There was no sensation of moving or anything. I don't know if we moved. I don't know. After it was all over we couldn't believe it and knew we couldn't convince people of what we seen and we waited a while before we went to the Sheriff's Department and told them. I wanted to get the military in on it. I didn't want any publicity and I didn't want any news people, but after I thought about it awhile I figured that was what I should do.

Derrington: What time would you say elapsed from the beginning until you were released?

Hickson: Oh, it had to be - it's hard to say.

Derrington: Was it hours or minutes?

Hickson: It had to be an hour or so. It had to be that long, but it seemed like an eternity. As far as I know I was conscious but I had no sensations inside of there — I didn't have any power to move.

Derrington: How were you released?

Hickson: They carried me right back out and I was immediately put on the, .ground. I felt no pain and I felt normal. Then the vehicle was gone.

Derrington: During this time do you recall seeing Mr. Parker?

Hickson: I don't recall seeing him until after I was out.

Derrington: You didn't see him onboard?

Hickson: No, sir, I didn't. I don't recall seeing him on board at all. As I said, I was scared partly out. of my mind.

Derrington: When was the first time you noticed Calvin?

Hickson: When they brought me back out on the ground, I believe, is when I seen him again. He was hysterical and sort of looked like he was paralyzed but he suddenly came to his senses.

Derrington to Parker: Before you passed put, do you recall being lifted into the vehicle?

Parker: I recall them getting me and just like a big magnet drawing me to it. I wasn't on the ground — I was off the ground. I don't remember a thing. I just blacked out. I just stood there like I was froze. Then I finally got to where I could move a little bit. It was like a bad dream. I wish it had been a bad dream and it would all be over with. I didn't sleep more than three seconds all night.

Derrington: Do you bringing you back out?
recall them

Parker: No, sir. When I came to the ship went 'zzzp' and disappeared.

Derrington: Did you discuss what had happened between you?

Parker: I passed out. I did not remember anything.

Hickson: We discussed what had happened to me. We talked a while trying to decide what to do. We drove to a quick service store and discussed it for almost an hour before we decided to go to the Sheriff's office...

Derrington: Did you have anything to drink any place that someone could have slipped something into your drink?

Hickson: No, sir, because we didn't stop anywhere. I had frozen shrimp that was in the freezer that we were fishing with. We didn't stop anywhere but went straight to the river.

Derrington: What is the relationship between the two of you?

Hickson: He is just a friend. His father and myself back home were real good friends, almost like brothers, and he's been down a couple of weeks now working at the same place that I work...

Derrington: Did you hear any other sounds beside this buzzing sound that you mentioned earlier?

Hickson: The only sound that I heard was one of the things made some type of noise. It wasn't anything that I could distinguish or understand.

Parker: It was just a "mmm."

Derrington: Any dust or....

Hickson: No, sir. I didn't see any dust or anything.

Parker: I don't know how to explain it. It was just as still like, and everything, and then I heard a 'zzzp' just like that, and looked around and blue lights coming, and I paralyzed right there. You know, just like if you walk outside and step on a rattlesnake.

Think how you feel. That is just how I felt. I would rather it had been a rattlesnake.

Derrington: No depressions in the area at all after this?

Hickson: No, sir.

Parker: Something else. The craft — it never did set down on the ground itself. It stayed approximately two feet from it.

Hickson: It was off the ground.

Parker: Well, really, they didn't nothing touch it — the ground....

Derrington: No exhaust or anything?

Hickson: I didn't see it. If it was I didn't see it. But as I said, I was quite scared.

Derrington: No attempt to your knowledge to communicate with you in any way?

Hickson: Only unless it was — I don't think it was trying to communicate with us. I think — I don't know — it might have been communicating with the others but I didn't hear any —

Parker: They didn't act like they meant any harm to us.

Hickson: They didn't harm me I know, that I know of.

Parker: They did me physically right now but, you know, not physically but mentally it is about to tear me up.

Derrington: What about curiosity. Did there appear to be any unusual curiosity about the objects?

Hickson: It seemed to me that they knew what they were doing, but they was — I don't know what they were trying to find out but they were trying to find out something about us because —you know — what they done to me, and I don't know what they were doing. Other than that, it seemed that they knew what they were doing.....

Derrington: Is this the first experience of this nature that you have had?

Hickson: Yes, sir. This is the first I have ever had of that nature.

Derrington: Prior to this, have you read or heard about unidentified flying objects?

Hickson: Oh yes. I've read and I've heard. Yes, sir. .

Parker: Not too long ago — now it hadn't been — how long? In the apartments? .

Hickson: Yeah. Not too long ago in Gautier there was one of these.

Parker: And there was at least 13 or 14witnesses.

Hickson: A dozen families was watching it.

Derrington: But this is the first time you have seen anything like this?

Hickson: Like that, yes, sir.

Derrington: You have never seen anything in the past at a distance that you thought —

Hickson: A while back, there was a dozen families out there that said it could have been a flying object. You know — I don't know if it was a flying object or not.

Derrington: You saw something though?

Parker: Yes, sir. There was about 13more that did.

Hickson: But it was — what they —what we were looking at that night was a glow. It was a real red glowing thing. It could have been a pier light, I guess —or something like that. But I've never, had any experiences with other things close to something like that.

Derrington: Now,' back to , the description of the object. You said about 8 feet in diameter and ;about —

Hickson: It's a rough guess. I mean, I'd say that there wasn't enough of an area in there that they would have — too many things couldn't have been in there.

Derrington: No protrusion or anything similar to a wing of an aircraft?

Hickson: No, sir. I didn't see anything.

Parker: I could sketch a picture out of the craft itself — you know, just on the outside. The inside I can't, now.

Hickson:. It wasn't round, it was more or less oblong, or something like that. It wasn't completely round.

Derrington: Did you ever hear any motor sounds?

Hickson: Nothing but just the little buzzing is all that I heard.

Derrington: Did it buzz all of the time or just when it moved?

Hickson: No, sir. When it moved. Inside of it I didn't hear any sound from the vehicle or whatever it was. I didn't hear any sound from it while I was in there.

Derrington: About how tall were these things?

Hickson: Well, it's hard to tell about everything. It had to — it was tall enough that when we went in the opening we wasn't touching anything.

Derrington: I mean the individuals.

Hickson: I'd say somewhere approximately 5 feet, or something like that.

Parker: Of course you know they wasn't on the 'ground so that made them taller than us. You know — as far as getting out walking across, the ground.

Hickson: When you are that frightened it's hard to give a good description of something. .

Derrington: You talked about them moving. Did they move with leg motion or —

Parker: Drifted.

Hickson: Just flying. .

Parker: Like if wasn't no gravity around.

Hickson: I didn't see any motion of their legs but I know they had motion with what I guess was arms — I guess it was arms because they moved them whenever they lifted me.

Parker: And it was like a crawfish or crab.

Derrington: Was anything strapped on this, like a sort of pack or anything?

Hickson: I didn't see anything like that.. Just the thing, is all.

Derrington: Just the body frame of the individual and it was either unclothed or clothed with something very tight fitting?

Hickson: Yes.

Derrington: Did this creature have two arms and two legs, or what seemed to be?

Hickson: It seemed to be two of each one. Yes, sir.

Parker: But it wasn't like our arms and legs. You know, well it was on the same basic manner as an arm and leg but it wasn't physically looking the same.

Huntley: I believe you told me that it looked more like a crab claw.

Parker: Yes sir.

Hickson: The guy had claw like things. It wasn't fingers like our fingers are....

Derrington: Were there any windows in the craft?

Hickson: I couldn't see anything from inside of it. I don't know...

Derrington: Did it go straight up?

Parker: No sir. It just disappeared... 'zzzp' and it just disappeared.

Hickson: And really, I don't know how it got there.

Major Winans: Did it seem to be plastic, or transparent, or was it solid looking material?

Hickson: It had a glow and I couldn't tell whether it was solid or transparent. I couldn't give you no details of that at all because I don't know.

Winans: Was it glowing from the inside or from the outside?

Hickson: It was glowing — it was bluish like on the outside and on the inside it was just like — you know, like light.

Winans: Just like in this room herewith the fluorescent color? Same color?

Hickson: Yes, only there was no bulbs, globes, or anything.

Winans: Did you feel the same temperature, or did you feel warm?

Hickson: I didn't have any sensation —any feeling at all.

Amdall: Did you feel like you could have moved?

Hickson: I couldn't move.

Derrington: What went on while you were inside?

Hickson: Well, then — as I said before, they had something — I still say an eye— which I know it wasn't an eye — but, it just circulated around — around by me — and they could do me any way they wanted to — lay me back, or sideways.

Derrington: This eye that was under you — you were under constant observation by this eye while you were on the board?

Hickson: Yes. I say an eye. I don't mean it in that respect. Well, when something is looking at me like that I guess you would figure you would have to say it's some kind of an eye. It didn't look like a camera or anything like that. Huntley: Now when you were stretched out — I believe you said you were stretched out. Right?

Hickson: At one time, yes, sir.

Huntley: Did you say — didn't you tell us that they moved the light over you —back and forth and all over your body?

Hickson: The thing moved all back over me and all around me.

Derrington: Did it move by itself?

Hickson: It moved by itself to the best I can remember. I was so darned scared till I don't really know whether I lost consciousness. I don't think I did. I don't think I lost consciousness. I think I was conscious all the time — I believe I was — that I was in there.

Winans: Did the projector have any sort of an arm to it?

Hickson: I don't know. It didn't seem to be attached to anything. It could have been. I don't know.

Derrington: When you regained consciousness, where did you go first? After you left this area?

Hickson: Well, we went over across —we live in Gautier. We stopped over there at the — close to the Li'l General Curb Market and talked about it a longtime again.

Derrington: What time was this now?

Hickson: Oh, this must have been —aw heck, it was around 10 or 11 o'clock, or something like that.

Huntley: They came into the Sheriff's office at, I believe, 11:18...

Amdall: Have either of you been on any medication or any kind of drugs?

Hickson: No, sir.

Parker: No, sir. I haven't.

Derrington: What about alcohol?

Parker: I don't drink.

Hickson: Well, I take a drink occasionally and after that happened last night — after I left the Sheriff's Department, I got home and I even took a drink to try to relax and it didn't even relax me. I drink occasionally', yes.

Derrington: But you had had nothing to drink prior to this?

Hickson: No, sir.

Winans: How did you get that mark on the tip of your little finger?

Hickson: This is a blister, you know —from some hot steel. No, it is not related to this at all.

Huntley: Calvin had a couple of little small scratches on this right arm. When he mentioned something about a claw and I noticed that he said he grabbed him by both arms and I noticed that both arms have a little scratch.

Hickson: Well, I couldn't find any scratches at all on me. There's no marks at all that I — I didn't find any on me at all.

Parker: There wasn't no feeling to the thing. You just couldn't feel nothing. It's a wonder I didn't hurt myself when I came through this.

Attorney Colingo: I can say this. Not this particular story, but at the same time, this object was sighted by others who are as critical or — well by officers. One man was Broadus. He related the story again this morning at the police station where they were going down the highway and passed the vicinity where. they were. You can see it from the, highway there just across the bridge. They saw the object for three minutes. And the times correspond. . .;

Huntley: And their description and everything. They even described the blue lights and everything.

Hanson: Was it a dark blue light or a light blue light?

Hickson: It was just a glowing... don't know.

Colonel Rudolph: Had they had the opportunity to hear the tape before reporting this?

Huntley: Yes.

Colingo: Oh, they have heard it now. Do you mean did they know?

Huntley: Yes. The tape — I took the tape, or they did, last night: I played it back...

Rudolph: Before they gave their report?

Colingo: Did Broadus come and report this sighting and then these men?

Huntley: I don't remember now. I would have to check with the chief on that. But I do know that they heard the tape that we took last night — or they took last night.

Rudolph: This was after they had been in to tell their story?

Huntley: Right. Then that is when they said, "Well, you know that is funny because we saw the same thing. We saw a blue light." In fact Mr. Broadus is a Christian man and he said he'd been over to Gautier somewhere to church.

Colingo: If Mr. Broadus says he saw it— he saw it. I mean, he is that type of fellow. Now this other fellow — I don't know who you are talking about.

THE END

For more details on alien abduction please visit:

http://www.amazon.com/dp/B00GPYEV9G

For more details on UFO's and aliens please visit:

http://www.amazon.com/dp/B00BL2MPNG

Printed in the USA
CPSIA information can be obtained
at www.ICGtesting.com
CBHW072256111224
18869CB00009B/455